NORTH CORNWALL
CAMERA
Ray Bishop

BOSSINEY BOOKS

First published in 1994
by Bossiney Books, St Teath, Bodmin, Cornwall.

Typeset and printed by
Penwell Ltd, Callington, Cornwall.

Copyright 1994 Ray Bishop and Michael Williams

ISBN 0948158 97 2

ACKNOWLEDGEMENTS
Front cover: Ray Bishop
Back cover: Ray Bishop
Front cover design: Maggie Ginger

Front cover: 'TIME gentlemen please!' This dog, belonging to Sam Treglown, the then landlord of The Swan at Wadebridge, is called to the bar. Sam was a well-known sportsman in North Cornwall and his son John played Rugby for Cornwall.

Introducing
RAY BISHOP and his Photographs

Ray Bishop is a photographer for all seasons. Cornish born and bred, Ray started serious professional photography back in 1951, and he has gone on providing a highly professional service for all types of publisher for more than four decades. It was my then editor Brenda Duxbury who introduced Ray to Bossiney, the year was 1977 and we needed a cover for *Along the Camel*. Brenda took me to meet him at his home, Mulberry Cottage in Molesworth Street, Wadebridge. He not only produced the right cover, a highly evocative colour transparency of Padstow Harbour, but showed me some beautiful black and white photographs.

Immediately, I knew I was in the presence of a man with rare vision and sensitivity. There was a lyrical shot of swans on the river, the town bridge in the background – it made the perfect opening photograph for that early Bossiney title.

Since that evening he has gone on taking pictures for us – more than two thousand of them, and in all those years I have never seen a bad Ray Bishop photograph. In many Bossiney publications, he has been essentially co-author, his images drifting beautifully, evocatively, across the pages.

Ray has produced photographs for both local and national newspapers and magazines – on one famous occasion every photograph which appeared in the *Cornish Magazine* was his. In 1981 he scooped for Fleet Street the dramatic, tragic shooting of a Securicor guard outside a Wadebridge bank.

I have never asked him why he didn't go to London and the big time. I guess he loved Cornwall too dearly. Like Dr Jonathon Couch of Polperro and Dr William Borlase down in West Cornwall, he has remained loyal to Cornwall. Pope once wrote of Borlase 'In

3

■ *SWANS and cygnets on the River Camel at Wadebridge.*

The bridge has been in constant use for more than five centuries. Carew, whose Survey of Cornwall gives us a picture of Cornwall in Elizabethan times, rated it 'the longest, the strongest and the fairest that the shire can muster.' During the Civil War, none less than Oliver Cromwell came with fifteen hundred Roundheads to take command of the bridge. With columns of well-trained horses and disciplined men, they must have made an impressive sight. By tradition, the ford at Wadebridge was so dangerous that a chapel was erected on each bank enabling travellers on one side to pray for a safe crossing, and on the other to offer up thanks. Around 1470, the Vicar of Egloshayle, Thomas Loveybond, raised money to build the much-needed bridge, but when work was underway difficulties were encountered – a matter of finding sufficiently strong foundations for the piers. Legend – and there is no shortage of legendary explanation in North Cornwall – says the problem was solved by building on wool-packs.

the shade, but shining,' and the same could be said of Ray Bishop.

The camera can, in fact, do a whole album of things. The camera can capture and record, can skim a surface or probe a subject. It can be a joke or a reliable witness. But everything, of course, depends on the man holding the camera: his craft, his vision and ability to select. Ray knows all this, as if by instinct. Much of his press work by its very nature is in the form of groups and posed photographs, but he is a real all-rounder. Out on our varied Cornish landscapes, he understands subtleties and changes of mood. On the cricket field he can freeze the poetry of a classical cover drive or the stumps shattered by a fierce fast delivery. As a keen sportsman I have also admired his photographs of Cornish wrestling and Rugby – yes, a real all-rounder – and as a member of the Ghost Club Society I hope he will, one day, photograph a ghost, proving the reality of psychic phenomena. That would be a great moment.

Inside these pages Ray concentrates his camera on North Cornwall, but for Bossiney he has photographed a whole range of subjects inside Cornwall and beyond the Tamar: Arthurian sites in Somerset, legendary locations in Devon, places off the beaten track in Dorset – he has even photographed me sitting at Hitler's desk! – and haunted properties all over our publishing territory.

Ray Bishop is as North Cornish as the River Camel or Rough Tor. His father came from Bodieve, a hamlet just outside Wadebridge, and his mother from the fishing village of Port Isaac. He was born at Wadebridge and educated at the old Bodmin Grammar School 'where I played for my house at cricket and football, and particularly liked athletics, being often a winner in the sprints.'

'Going to school I used to pass the old Drill Hall which displayed a poster encouraging passers-by to 'Join the Army and see the World. Little did I think that in just a few years this was going to happen to me!

'With geography and history amongst my favourite school subjects I was very interested to visit cities such as Durban, Bombay, Baghdad, Tehran, Cairo and Beirut, all quite peaceful at that time during, and just after, World War Two.

'Travelling with an Army rail party across France, I saw from the train, through an early morning mist, the walls and towers of

Carcassonne and resolved to visit it sometime to explore and photograph. This I was able to do during a car tour of Southern France in 1955. Switzerland is another country that has excellent opportunities for photographs … Spain and Southern Italy also offer good subjects for the camera'.

Between 1942 and 47, he served as a cipher operator in the Royal Corps of Signals, doing service in South Africa, India, Iraq, Iran, the Lebanon, Syria, Egypt, Jordan and Palestine. 'This involved some very interesting work concerning top secret messages about Russian spies.'

He then spent 30 years as an administrator in the Health Service, combining it with part-time photography. It was in 1981 that he turned to full-time photography.

'I had my very first camera in 1939. No, I didn't take photographs as a young boy. There was an aunt, my mother's sister, who took most of the family photographs.'

He bought his cottage in Molesworth Street in 1955, and the adjoining land, which had been a builder's yard. The coach house and stables of earlier days remain, 'but the builders had laid a foot of hardcore … they needed a hard surface for their vehicles. So there was a lot of hard work before it really became a garden.' The mock tower base in the garden today is a reminder of all that effort, transforming the area into a lovely town garden. In fact, it is difficult to believe you are in the middle of a town. Tamsin Thomas and I interviewed Ray for a BBC Radio Cornwall series here, and we both remarked on the fact you felt you were in a country garden.

Ray is an accomplished gardener. His activities include grafting fruit trees, and he has won many awards in the fruit classes at shows. 'I only enter fruit classes,' he says, and the garden is living evidence of his talents: apples and pears, currants, red, white and black, strawberries and raspberries – 'and mulberries in a good year.'

Naturally Wadebridge is the window of Ray's world, but photographically he knows Cornwall better than anybody else today. He has explored the moors of Penwith, discovered and rediscovered the subtleties of the Lizard peninsula and the Roseland, traced the Tamar from its source to the Sound, visited dozens of churches – and a great deal more.

He is a master at capturing atmosphere. One of our bestselling titles is Peter Underwood's *Ghosts of Cornwall,* and Ray produced the perfect cover: a ghostly monk in grey walking through haunted St Nectan's Glen near Tintagel. Alas, it's not a genuine spectre, but such is Ray's craft and professionalism that I've been asked many times: 'Is it a real ghost?'

■ *RAY recalls: 'I set out to deliver some photographs to Wadebridge School when suddenly I met fellow photographer and friend Hilda Hambly who said "Isn't it terrible?" She went on to explain a man had been shot: part of a hold-up of the Securicor van which had just arrived outside the Midland Bank. The odd thing is the van parked in this side street, but was, in fact, delivering to the Barclays Bank just up the street. My photograph shows the security man's body lying covered in the road, and others taking the money around the corner to Barclays. Kay Pope, a girl from Blisland, showing great courage, chased the hold-up man and was shot in the leg. I saw her being carried away on a stretcher but did not think it a suitable photograph. This photograph, though, appeared in some London and Bristol newspapers.'*

7

The close-up of the black cat for *Superstition and Folklore*, the beautiful coastline at Trevalga with potter Heather Swain in the foreground for *E V Thompson's Westcountry*, and looking across the harbour for our *About Boscastle* are just three more examples of his ability to produce the right cover picture.

'I'm a completely self-taught photographer,' Ray recalls. 'I can still remember those first photographs I took back in 1939. A schoolboy friend and I decided to visit Brown Willy, and I took my new camera. We cycled to Jamaica Inn and then walked the rest of the way. There was a professional photographer living and working in Wadebridge at the time: Mr Arthur Shepherd who developed and printed photographs for local people. He complimented me on these photographs, their composition and exposure...and that was the beginning.

'I didn't do any photography during my Army years. One was warned not to have a camera among your personal possessions, and I stuck to the rules.

'One of my earliest photographs to be published in the *Cornish Guardian* showed Lower Treneague Cottage near Wadebridge with its camomile lawn. The owner of the property, Miss Dorothy Sewart, later produced the camomile commercially and sold it in this country and abroad, incuding the United States of America. I took numerous photographs of the plants and lawns for her. Mr Norman Lyne, the editor, phoned me to say he liked the pictures I had sent and asked me to continue sending in photographs which I have done for some forty years. Then when the *Cornish Guardian* changed its policy and the front page small advertisements gave way to news the very first picture on that front page was my shot of Port Isaac Town Platt taken looking over a wall in Fore Street.'

Ray takes pride in the fact that when his daughter Wenna and son Piran took their degrees, they chose art and for their second subject they both selected photography.

A former President of the Wadebridge Camera Club, and a member for something like forty years. Ray has a wonderful knack handling old photographs. When I began publishing a friend advised: 'Don't ever copy old pictures . . . they lose their quality in the process.' But meeting this man changed all that: his reproduction of often quite ancient photographs is remarkable. 'I rely on daylight,'

■ *A VERY SKILFUL piece of photography by Ray. This little boy from near St Issey was celebrating his fourth birthday, and Ray arranged these four candles in front of a mirror. It has been said that a candle can predict the future. If, for example, it is reluctant to light, then a storm is on its way. Anyway, this carefully planned photograph is a real triumph.*

says Ray, 'not artifical light.'

One writer who knows Ray Bishop well is Sarah Foot. She has written on a variety of themes for Bossiney and recently contributed a perceptive Introduction to our 225th title *Secret Devon*. Here are her thoughts on the man and his craft.

'Over a period of some ten years or more I was involved in writing books about Cornwall and its countryside, and people both past and present.

'During this time it was my good fortune to share many of my explorations with Ray Bishop who came with me to photograph some of the places and people I was to see and meet.

'Always the professional, he would manage without any fuss or bother to have the right equipment for any given occasion and to capture the atmosphere of a place or the character of a person with easy perfection.

9

'A quiet and mild man, he felt as enthusiastic as I did about my Cornish discoveries and was often able to introduce me to secret places and wonderful vistas I might not have found otherwise, and then to photograph them in a most imaginative way.

'We must have travelled hundreds of miles together over the lesser-known routes of Cornwall, visiting river banks, churches, grand houses, cottages and barren moorland, and we must have sat talking for many hours with Cornish people of all ilks, from farmers, fishermen, ferrymen, restaurateurs, writers, painters and the gentry. Ray was always a good partner on all these forays and always managed to bring these places and people to life in his photographs.

'It was a great bonus for me to have such a companion, someone who was never intrusive but always interested, sympathetic and inquisitive. His photographs are proof of his professional capacity and his depth of feeling for people and places and his insight into atmosphere and differing dimensions.'

Someone else who has travelled many miles on photographic expeditions is Felicity Young of Tintagel. Felicity is another all-rounder, combining painting and photography, book illustrating and writing; outside and beyond all that, she is a keen horsewoman and a qualified yoga teacher.

'When I think of Ray and his photography,' she says, 'I think of climbing hedges, walls, stepladders . . . nothing is too difficult or too tricky for Ray. He has used me as the figure in the picture on a number of occasions: looking through the telescope at Land's End and the Lizard, riding my horse Red, painting a picture at Tintagel, looking at a Barbara Hepworth sculpture at St Ives . . . for that photograph he stood on a wall with a petrifying drop.

'We've travelled hundreds of miles to get the right photographs, and when you're the model you know *precisely* where to stand . . . not orders, but you're politely guided as to your position . . . and he doesn't keep his subjects hanging about too long on a cold morning.

◀ *THE PHOTOGRAPHER is often an artist in his own right.*

'Looking through doors and down passageways, he is an imaginative photographer and he's skilful in the way he uses a figure or an animal in the landscape, giving a sense of perspective.

'Above all, he knows what he's looking for. He begins the day with a very good idea of the things he intends to photograph, though, of course, he sees unscheduled things during the day, and it's then that his ability to seize the moment comes to the fore. Ray makes good use of what happens and what he sees, and then there's this great clarity about many of his photographs. Sometimes too there is a lovely sense of humour in his photograhy. Just look at that dog in the bar and you'll see what I mean. And unlike many photographers, he handles colour and black and white with equal skill. Whichever way you look at Ray, he's a fine photographer.'

Felicity touches on an important matter when she refers to the 'happenings' on a day of photography. The man and his horses ploughing the field, the girl bunching flowers for the market, the train travelling on its journey, *happen* to Ray. All these things are not only activity, they have a certain awareness – and these are the qualities which he captures in his photographs. In a way, he's a kind of visual historian.

On the subject of history, how many people know the Westcountry is the cradle of the camera? Thomas Wedgewood of Dorset, who died in 1805 at the age of 34, with his discovery still imperfect, was the pioneer. By the time of his tragically early death, Wedgewood had already founded photography on the principle of making pictures by the action of light.

And Ray in his quiet perceptive style is part of this great Westcountry tradition, capturing people, places and events on film.

His older photographs are especially evocative. The fact is what was Ray's working day has become part of our North Cornwall heritage.

Long may he click his camera.

Michael Williams
Bossiney Books

■ *RAY Bishop wins 'Photographer of the Year' award at the Wadebridge Camera Club in April 1990. The award is presented by the judge Charles Hoskin of Camborne. Two of Ray's splendid portrait prints are in the background; these were his winning shots in the colour and monochrome prints of the year competitions. The gentleman in the left-hand photograph is Mike Grigg of St Issey who had just become President of the Camera Club, and the young girl on the right is the daughter of Trevor England of Padstow, a RNLI celebrity in North Cornwall.*

The celebrated French photographer Henri Cartier-Bresson once said 'Photography is the spontaneous impulse which comes from perpetually looking, and which seizes the instant and its eternity.' Ray, in his own way, does precisely that. His best pictures have a distinct quality, reflecting a sense of place that is, as has been said of Sir John Betjeman, both varied and tender. There is beauty and a sense of geometry about many of them. He has an instinct, almost an intuition, for the decisive moment. This is especially true in his action shots, notably on the sports field.

■ *A SPLENDID example of Ray's ability to seize the moment – and freeze it. He came to Demelza, a hamlet of one and a half acres off the road which strides across the Goss Moor. Suddenly this character came down the lane, a Saturday morning in December 1983, and Ray snapped his shutter. The distinguished novelist Winston Graham, creator of the* **Poldark** *novels, used the name Demelza for his heroine. On the small screen in the memorable television series Angharad Rees, the beautiful Welsh actress, played Demelza: a miner's daughter brought up in squalor and poverty, being transformed into a gentleman's wife. Hers was a role of incredible contrast and growth, from a fourteen-year-old waif to maturity. Winston Graham, who lived and wrote in Cornwall for some years, is acknowledged as one of the greatest novelists in the world. Richard Church in* **Country Life** *wrote 'He is a master of the art of pure story-telling...'.*

The chapel on the left of Ray's photograph was opened in 1871.

■ TAMSIN Thomas presenting a copy of her new book *Mysteries of the South West*, to the Mayor of Bodmin, Councillor Captain E T Denholm, RN retired, at Bricknells of Bodmin. On the left is Martin Bricknell. This, Bossiney's 211th title, containing a good deal of Bodmin Moor subject matter, prompted book reviewer Ronnie Hoyle in the *North Cornwall Advertiser* to write 'There is little doubt that Tamsin Thomas has become the "Voice of Cornwall" but now she is fast becoming the county's investigator of mysteries as well.' It was also well reviewed by Dr James Whetter who in *The Cornish Banner* said 'The enchantment, the spiritual emanations of some of Cornwall's most interesting sites are brilliantly explored while Ray Bishop's photographs add greatly to one's understanding and appreciation.' In her opening chapter Tamsin writes: 'There's nothing more exciting than to discover a hidden mystery in the landscape and like Dame Daphne du Maurier in her explorations in *Vanishing Cornwall* there have been times when I've wanted to shout "Eureka!" – indeed, sometimes I did. Feel free to do the same. It's not quite like planting a flag on some newly discovered pinnacle, but it does fill you with a sense of achievement.'

■ *TIMES were when the sight and sound of trains was a reasonably frequent occurrence in the Cornish countryside, but Dr Beeching and the motor car have changed the scene. Here are photographs of the old Boscarne to Wenford line back in 1962. Normally passengers did not use this old line. It was employed to move china clay and granite. However, on this May day, a special train, made up of guards' vans, ran for this one special trip – and Ray has a reminder of that journey: his return ticket of five shillings and sixpence.*

Below are the British Rail personnel involved with this one-off journey. The driver on the left is Bob Irons, a Wadebridge sportsman who went on to captain Wadebridge Cricket Club.

The photograph on the left shows the train on the move with local businessman Doug Lang waving to friends. The choice of guards' vans was a necessity because only these could negotiate the sharp bends of the track.

■ IT IS a tragedy that Cornwall has never been able to support professional theatre on a permanent basis. We have the magical Minack Theatre near Land's End, but for regular professional theatre we have to cross the Tamar and go to the Theatre Royal, a magnificent modern theatre in Plymouth.

However, amateur theatrical groups abound in North Cornwall, and one of the most active is the Camhayle Theatre Club, based at Wadebridge, which prides itself on putting on plays which range from farce to Shakespeare. Over the years, their dedication to the theatre has earned them the reputation of being 'professional amateurs' – they are only amateurs by virtue of the fact that they do not act full-time! This photograph was taken when the group took part in the annual Wadebridge Carnival and illustrates some of the plays the group has put on over the years – Night Must Fall, Bedroom Farce, King Doniert, Twelfth Night, Blithe Spirit and the hilarious Halfway up the Tree. In the picture are (from left to right): Jem Marshall (current chairman) of Polmorla Road, Wadebridge: Liz King (now 'up country'), Mike Clarke, Joan Franklin, Chris Ridley (who is also connected to Bodmin Folk Club); Carole Wreyford, Mike Parry, Ann Gell (now with Phoenix Players of Bodmin), Ronnie Hoyle, June and John Holmes (who is also president of Camelford Amateur Operatic Society!).

■ *Woods are magical places, especially in autumn, many curiously generate the air of a place untrodden. This is a wonderful setting near Golitha Falls down the Fowey Valley. The branches of these beeches show the sculptural quality in nature. 'I came to these woods in 1979 with the writer Sarah Foot who was then working on her first book for Bossiney. It was about the River Fowey and we travelled from its early beginnings on the moor all the way down to Fowey where it meets the sea,' says Ray. It is interesting to reflect how trees and woods have fired the creative chemistry of painters, writers and photographers. To the early people in history the forests around them must have seemed mysterious locations and, in a way, many woods retain that mysterious quality today. That great expert of the countryside Gilbert White rated beech 'the loveliest of all forest trees.' It's certainly one of the strongest British timbers and has been used for many household items.*

Ray modestly admits: 'I suppose this is a good photograph. I was lucky to be there at that time and, of course, that lovely long branch helps to make the picture.'

■ THE beaches of North Cornwall are great tourist assets, places enjoyed by locals too.

Here are two different faces of the beach scene – opposite two young ladies discuss the merits of surf boards at Constantine Bay. One resident surfer says 'You have this good mixture of relaxation *and* excitement. It's a sport with a difference.' The sport really took off in Cornwall in the 1970s.

Below, visitors come ashore at Rock by ferry. This ferry which has been running between Rock and Padstow since 1337 was known as Black Tor Rock or Black Tor Passage and belonged to the Duchy Manor of Penmayne. Now operated by the Padstow Harbour Commissioners, who use powerful motor launches, it was originally propelled by oar and sail.

Enid Harvey who lived in Padstow most of her life, coming to Rock in latter years, recalled her father Dr Harvey who practised, like his father-in-law before him, in Padstow, living at Rosehill at the top of the town. He had a surgery in Rock, but if a patient wanted him in an emergency at night, a fire was lit on the beach and he came across by boat – or if it was too rough then it was four-teen miles round the estuary through Wadebridge with horse and trap.

■ PATRICK Eagar, generally rated the most perceptive photographer in world cricket today, once said 'Let the action happen ... ' Ray does precisely that during a Minor Counties championship match on the Wadebridge ground. Cornwall are in the field and Ray captures the action of the bowler Peter Kendall as he follows through, and the keen anticipation of the three Cornish fielders in the picture. They are – left to right – Bruce Nicholls of Gerrans, Robin Harvey, the Cornwall captain, and Gerald Tregunna moving in from cover.

Robin Harvey, the son of a St Columb veterinary surgeon, was educated at Blundells, Tiverton: a public school which has produced many notable sportsmen, including fellow Cornishman Richard Sharp who captained England at rugby. Robin, a powerful hitter of the ball, more than one six from his bat on this ground landed in the River Camel! A positive captain who led by example, Robin's emigration to South Africa was a big blow to Cornish cricket. His father Geoffrey Harvey played cricket for Cornwall – as did Peter Kendall's father. Charles Kendall, a Cornish policeman, was rated a very fine new ball bowler.

■ THE SOUTH African-born England test cricketer Basil d'Oliveira signing for young autograph hunters on the Wadebridge ground in 1953. The previous day d'Oliveira had scored a rapid century guesting for the Cornish Crusaders at Helston. Interestingly, the young man on the left, Richard Isbell of Liskeard went on to become the secretary of the Cornish Crusaders, and has been a notable captain for the club. d'Oliveira, a greatly respected all-round cricketer and man, was at the centre of a political storm when the South African authorities refused him entry to their country as a member of the England team on account of his coloured skin. As a result, England declined to tour and South Africa went in the sporting wilderness for many years. With one of the shortest backlifts in the game, Basil d'Oliveira's timing and power, particularly off the back foot, were tremendous. People who saw his batting for the Crusaders still talk about it.

■ *CORNISH wrestling has a long history. Historians tell us at the Battle of Agincourt, where the banners depicted the different contingents, the Cornishmen had two wrestlers on theirs. An excellent wrestler – or 'wrastler' as we Cornish put it, was Richard Trevithick, who by the age of twenty-five invented a high pressure steam engine. The Greeks of long ago, who wrestled at the Isthmian and Olympic Games, found it a slippery business in that they smeared their bodies with grease and wrestled in the nude! Cornish wrestlers, in comparison, are substantially clad. They wear a wrestling jacket, made of sturdy sailcloth, with short loose sleeves, and fastened at the front by cords; shorts and some even don socks – as this picture confirms. 'Action photography on sporting occasions is a matter of precise, very precise timing. A few seconds more and this man would have been on the ground,' says Ray Bishop.*

■ A RAY BISHOP milestone: celebrating the taking of his 1,000th photograph for Bossiney. 'I have to confess it was a shot taken across the Tamar in Devon, the Scorhill stone circle on Dartmoor. Sonia very kindly had this birthday cake especially made for the occasion.' Left to right: Michael Williams, Sonia Williams, Ray and author Sarah Foot. Ray has taken photographs for all Sarah's eight Bossiney titles. In late 1993 he took his 2,000th picture for the Cornish cottage publishers of St Teath: an empty sloping road high above the hamlet of Bossiney hard by Tintagel – on the surface nothing very remarkable but a phantom black dog has been seen on this stretch of road by a number of people over a number of years. Ray has also done a high percentage of our modern covers, all the eight covers on the circular table are his. The impact of a book's cover plays an enormously important part in the sales of a publication. Another vital factor in the packaging of a publication is the choice of the back cover photograph, which together with accompanying 'blurb' makes the title appealing to the eyes of a potential buyer.

■ ROBIN Ellis, who played the leading role of Ross Poldark in both BBC's television series of Poldark, climbs steps at ruined Tintagel Castle. His fictional role was several-sided: in turn masterful, rebellious, romantic, and, above all, headstrong. Even when he becomes, in fiction, a Cornish Member of Parliament, Ross Poldark does so on his terms, siding with the oppressed and fighting for what is right and fair.

Here at Tintagel we are at the heart of the Arthurian legend in Cornwall. It is to Tintagel that we come for the birth of Arthur, and interestingly more and more people are coming to the view that Arthur was an historical probability rather than a purely legendary character. Another interesting fact links this majestic headland to two great European legends: King Arthur and Tristan and Isolde. The connection between the two is reinforced when some accounts make Tristan a Knight of the Round Table.

Though the serious historian will argue Tintagel was built centuries *after* Arthur lived and fought the English, there is equally little doubt we had a King Arthur here in the Westcountry, and Tintagel is 'the garden of many Arthurian tales and his Court of Camelot.'

There is, too, something of a creative chemistry hereabouts. Otherwise how do we account for the many painters and writers who have attempted to pin Tintagel – and its qualities – on to canvas or paper?

Whether we believe in Arthur or not, Tintagel, for many, is a worthwhile destination, recharging the batteries and firing the imagination.

But here is a paragraph of warning from Felicity Young in *Tintagel Reflections:*

'King Arthur's Castle stands on what has become almost an island, only connected by a narrow neck of rock which is continually under attack from the wild Atlantic Ocean. A steep track, a bridge and over one hundred steps make the castle appear inhospitable but it is well worth the effort. To enjoy a visit to Tintagel Castle you must allow plenty of time. Too many visitors arrive in the village on a tight schedule and when they discover the castle is not the magnificent building which has caught their eye on the approach to Tintagel but merely a 'pile of stones' away on an island they are disappointed and go away without ever having set foot on the Castle Track.'

■ DOZMARY Pool frozen – and two rare photographs to prove it from early in 1963. A couple skating on the ice, and parked vans show just how solid the ice surface was in this very cold spell. The fact that these photographs were taken more than thirty years ago underlines the *relatively* mild nature of Cornish winters.

Curiously – or perhaps not so curiously – many Cornish tales feature water: the sea or a river or a lake. The moor is rich in folklore.

Standing on the rim of Dozmary you understand that breadth and space are dominant features in many of our Cornish landscapes – relying on basic elements of water, earth and sky. A mile in circumference, Dozmary Pool is a place of changing mood and beauty: a place of mystery and magic. The old people had an idea it was bottomless. In reality, Dozmary is surprisingly shallow. Often the pool becomes a mirror reflecting the forms of moor and cloud.

Some say Dozmary is where Sir Bedivere reluctantly threw away the magical sword Excalibur.

Sir John Betjeman once referred to 'a brooding melancholy at evening' over Dozmary. Bur spiritualists have come here to get in touch 'with the other side.'

Under normal conditions Dozmary is a beautiful sheet of water. On a diamond-sharp day it can sparkle like a jewel. Excalibur may not be lying out there, but you begin to understand how and why Dozmary has attracted painters and photographers – and appreciate how the place has triggered so many stories.

Dame Daphne du Maurier, of course, used this part of the Moor for her famous bestseller *Jamaica Inn*, first published in 1936 and rated by many Cornish people as their favourite novel.

■ *THOSE of us with good memories know the appeal of snow for children: the rarity and, above all, the fact that snow changes our everyday world into a **different** white world. Our moors get the worst of the snow – pretty to look at, perhaps, but a harsh fact of life for ponies and livestock and the reason why the RSPCA issues warnings about getting animals off the moorland in bad weather. Here is a photograph reflecting the happier side of being young in such weather. Two children build a snowchild on the edge of Bodmin Moor. Brown Willy, Cornwall's highest tor – a matter of 1,375 feet – stands in the background. They are Ray's son Piran and daughter Wenna. Piran today works for the archaelogical department of Exeter City Council. He was known in North Cornwall for his black and white pen drawings in the old **Gazette,** the forerunner of our **North Cornwall Advertiser.***

■ BOARDED shop windows in St Columb Major: a sure sign that it's Shrove Tuesday and time for Cornish hurling.

Hurling's origin lies deep in our Cornish past: vague and hazy like our landscape on a misty morning. Some believe it stems from the Bronze Age. Once a popular sport, it was condemned by the Puritans and, today, St Columb is its last Cornish stronghold.

An account of the sport by Richard Carew in 1602 uncannily anticipates some of Rugby's laws and patterns by more than two centuries. Consequently some of us in Cornwall feel we are justified in claiming that our hurlers were the real pioneers. It was only in 1823 that a boy, William Webb Ellis by name, picked up the ball and broke the law by running with it on the turf of Rugby School, thereby creating the modern game of Rugby.

Hurling differs from Rugby in that the object is to take the ball back to one's own goal or alternatively to run with the silver ball – and carry it over the parish boundary.

The ball itself, about the size of a cricket ball, is made of light wood and encased in silver, bearing the inscription:

'Town and Country, do your best

For in this parish I must rest.'

Ray's picture is a typical moment: hurlers of both teams waiting for the silver ball to fall.

■ JOE Halls was one of the great characters of Bodmin Moor.

Here he is photographed at Carkeet – he was then eighty years old – with Mr and Mrs Halls are their daughter Pam and granddaughter, Mary Marrack, and visiting author Sarah Foot at the back, wearing headscarf.

Ray says 'I've photographed many notable Cornish characters, and Joe Halls was one of the greatest.' At the time of this photograph he went to bed soon after dark as he only had candlelight. It was 1979. Joe was a life-long Methodist and told Sarah of the family walking to the St Luke's Chapel every Sunday: 'You could see the people coming down from the moor to chapel with lanterns and torches in their hands. My uncle walked several miles to chapel . . . sometimes two or three times a day. Their zeal shames us.'

Joe once went away on holiday. 'But everything was so flat there.' When he came back 'it was good to see the vozen and vain.'

'The vozen and the vain, the gorse and the bracken, his very breath of life,' Sarah wrote in her book *Following the River Fowey*.

John Wesley, of course, made enormous impact here in Cornwall. He hit Cornwall and the Cornish like a gale blowing in off the Atlantic, shattering old ideas and ancient values. He may have needed to stand on a stone to make himself heard, but he spoke a language our Cornish ancestors understood, and after Wesley came a whole army of Nonconformist preachers.

Wesley in all made six visits to Trewint on the edge of Bodmin Moor. On his first visit to Trewint in 1744, he wrote in his Journal 'wet and weary enough, having been battered by the rain and hail for hours.' (He travelled on horseback). 'I preached in the evening to more than the house would contain on the happiness of him whose sins are forgiven. In the morning Digory Isbell undertook to pilot us over the great moor, all the paths being covered with snow; which, in many places, was driven together too deep for man or horse to pass.'

■ RIDING remains the supreme way of exploring the moors of Cornwall. Here is the well-known Cornish broadcaster Tamsin Thomas of BBC Radio Cornwall. Tamsin says, 'It's an exhilarating experience. Riding somehow seems to add to the invigoration – and sense of journey.' On this occasion she is riding Moss Womble from the Moss Farm stables at Bradford on Bodmin Moor. They are at the Trippet or Dancing Stones on Manor Common, one of the lesser known stone circles.

Tamsin, who is the author of two Bossiney titles *Mysteries in the Cornish Landscape* and *Mysteries of the South West*, has a little ritual: 'I go around touching them all … a friendly stone has a warmth about it.'

Our stone circles remain great unsolved Cornish mysteries – nobody knowing their true purpose. There have been educated guesses but the real answer lies deep back in time – and will almost certainly remain there.

Ray reflects: 'Often horses and other animals are quite unpredictable, but this horse behaved pefectly, especially considering he had a strange rider in the saddle. And in this case you have a perfect model in Tamsin. No photographer could have asked for a better combination.'

■ *RAY says: 'Photography is often a matter of being in the right place at the right moment.' For the pilot of this light aircraft it was another matter. Ray had come to the Bodmin Airfield at Cardinham on a Sunday afternoon to do a publicity and press photograph of Bossiney books being flown to Dorset, when suddenly there was this aircrash at the edge of the airfield. Fortunately nobody was injured and Ray's photograph appeared in the* **Western Morning News.** *The other plane, carrying the Bossiney books and piloted by Richard Snow, was not involved in any way, and the following day some of those Bossiney titles were on sale in Dorset bookshops.*

■ THERE are probably more haunted properties in the Westcountry than anywhere in the United Kingdom outside London, and Ray has photographed many of them. Here is an interior shot of famous Jamaica Inn at Bolventor. Ghostly footsteps have paced this corridor.

Over the years a growing number of incidents at Jamaica Inn have defied reasonable logical explanation. These unexplained footsteps, the ghostly figure of a rider on horseback outside the inn, strange hoofbeats on the road and a ghost in a three-cornered hat in one of the bedrooms who finally disappeared through a large solid wardrobe. Earlier in the century too there was a stranger who stood drinking in the bar. He was called outside, but never returned to finish his drink. They found his murdered body next morning out on the moor. In the wake of that crime there was a volume of correspondence in *Country Life:* people claiming to see a strange man sitting on the wall outside the inn. Descriptions matched that of the murdered customer – and the general view was that the man sitting on the wall was, in fact, his ghost.

Ray is no cynic on the subject. He has heard phantom footsteps in a lane near St Breock Church, and, one day in a Wadebridge shop, he had a conversation with a man who was dead and buried.

He also has in his possession a photograph, taken by a former Cornish vicar, of a ghostly Elizabethan lady standing by a font in the vicar's church. The interesting thing here is when the photograph was taken, the *only* person in the building was the man with his camera.

Responsible investigators who have seen the picture are pretty sure it is a ghost. More and more students of the paranormal believe the 21st century may well produce scientific evidence proving the reality of psychic phenomena – and photographic evidence would be an important factor in providing that evidence.

■ MARIKA Hanbury Tenison loved Cornwall and, in some ways, was more Cornish than the Cornish.

She was an eminent journalist, author and broadcaster. She was an expert on food and had a great regard for Westcountry cooking: 'It has a richness unsurpassed in the British Isles,' she once said. Revelling in the access to fresh natural ingredients of the region – like the shellfish, the flat and deepsea fish, the game in the woods and the mushrooms in Cornish fields – she thought 'Westcountry food has a flair and flavour all of its own.'

There were also her books for children and her interest and knowledge of travel and primitive peoples – her husband was the explorer Robin Hanbury Tenison. Marika died of cancer at her home on Bodmin Moor on a Sunday morning in October 1982, aged only 44. Dr A L Rowse, writing in *the Western Morning News*, reflected 'With Marika Hanbury Tenison's death a light has gone out from Cornwall. Hers was a remarkable personality, gifted, gay, above all generous.'

Here she is posing for Ray with her typewriter outside her home at Cardinham, one of the last occasions she was photographed.

In the hope of helping fellow cancer sufferers, she made her serious – very serious – illness a public matter by appearing on BBC TV: a programme called *Quest for the Unicorn* in which she talked candidly about her condition. Viewers, like relations and close friends, were all impressed with her courage – not a hint of self-pity.

One curious fact of her practical and highly energetic life was her mythical love affair with unicorns – hence the name of the television programme. She was always convinced she would see one, either on the moor or in her water garden.

◀ *THROUGH his press work Ray has photographed a wide variety of sports. Here he is at the start of a road race from the Wadebridge sports centre: an excellent example of his ability to handle a crowded scene – the spectators and the runners.*

■ A STATELY avenue of trees. This narrow lane, just off the Camelford to Wadebridge road, leads on to Tredethy Country House Hotel. Set in nine acres of trees and shrubs and overlooking one of the most beautiful valleys in North Cornwall, Tredethy was once the home of royalty. When Prince Chula of Thailand was looking for a home in Cornwall he chose wisely. The Prince was a man of various roles. He owned and managed racing cars, driven by his cousin Prince Bira – they were well-known at Brooklands – but when he settled here in North Cornwall, he devoted himself to writing, broadcasting, lecturing and television work.

This area has triggered a good deal of paranormal activity. A phantom cyclist has been seen travelling along the Camelford-Wadebridge road. Ghostly figures have been observed inside the hotel – sometimes walking up the staircase at the level of the original one. The present staircase was built in 1868.

Ghosts, it would seem, take little notice of structural alterations to buildings; when they come back, they stick to old routes and ways. Outside the hotel, down in the valley, the ghost of Princess Chula has been witnessed by several people: no crunch of footsteps, just a silent figure. When we met Princess Narisa at Tredethy in October 1993, she told us that on the night her mother died she was seen by local residents on the other side of the valley.

When Sir John Betjeman came to this area in the 1930s researching and writing his first edition of *Cornwall, A Shell Guide*, he thought it looked 'like a Rowlandson landscape.' Thomas Rowlandson, who stayed with the Onslows at Hengar in the parish of St Tudy, sketched these wooded valleys, the tors on Bodmin Moor, our village churches, the farms and, of course, the North Cornish cliffs.

Mr Rowlandson may not have known it at the time, but he was setting a painting pattern. Other painters followed in his footsteps. So, though places like Newlyn and St Ives became the great artists' colonies, the tradition of painters coming to Cornwall started hereabouts.

■ IN THE summer of 1991 Bossiney reached a publishing milestone: the launching of the 200th title, and there was a celebration lunch at the Tredethy Country Hotel. Left to right: Peter Underwood, President of the Ghost Club Society, the man rated Britain's number one ghost hunter; Beryl Graham, proprietress of the hotel; Polly Lloyd of Bristol, television and radio broadcaster; David Mudd, author of the 200th title; Felicity Young of Tintagel, prolific illustrator for Bossiney; Elaine Beckton who lives near Truro and handles the publisher's advertising and Michael Williams. Some twenty-six years ago, in the belief that everyone is capable of writing one book, David Mudd set pen to paper. Not only was there one book, but it has been followed by thirteen solo books and five collaborations with other writers on themes ranging from personalities to places; from facts to mysteries; and from history to the off-beat.

He has now retired after 22 years as Member of Parliament for Falmouth and Camborne and he and his wife Diana now live just inside the Dartmoor National Park.

■ *ANCIENT and modern: in the foreground Stowe Barton, and on the skyline, the white saucers of the radar tracking station which remains something of a 'hush, hush' establishment in North Cornwall. Its official title is 'Composite Signals Organization Station.' As for Stowe Barton, this splendid farmhouse was built near the end of the eighteenth century, from materials left from the demolition of Stowe, once home of the famous Grenvilles. There is an odd and sad story mingling with the glory. John Grenville, son of Sir Bevil, played a major role in restoring the Stuart monarchy, and was handsomely rewarded for his efforts. He became Earl of Bath, Governor of Plymouth, Lord Lieutenant of Cornwall and a Privy Councillor. Such rewards sharpened his social ambitions, and Stowe was rebuilt in 1679. A fine building, four storeys high, boasting 365 windows, the great house stood for only a matter of six decades. A sequence of tragedy resulted in the last male heir departing this life in 1711. Sir Bevil's eldest daughter, for some reason, did not like Stowe, and ordered its demolition in 1739 – a ruthless method of avoiding the expense of running it.*

■ PHOTOGRAPHING animals can be a tricky business, but Ray has the patience and the skill – as these two photographs demonstrate. Above: equestrian conversation at the Royal Cornwall Show which is held annually at Wadebridge. Ray, in fact, was an active supporter of the campaign to stop the live export of British horses, ponies and donkeys for the dinner table in Europe.

Opposite: author E.V. Thompson and his son Luke (head and feet just visible from his perch behind the seat) being driven along the Fowey River road below Jamaica Inn at Bolventor by Jane Talbot-Smith. Times were when Bodmin Moor was known as Fowey Moor. The vehicle is drawn by Jane's horse Chateau Potensac, and the dog, a Dalmatian, is another of her animals. Jane Talbot-Smith and her husband Michael live alongside this lovely valley road. Her workshop is here too. A Master Saddler, in addition to saddlery and leather work she builds horsedrawn vehicles.

46

At one stage in her career she worked for Les Coker who made the side-saddle used by the Queen.

■ RAY has probably taken more photographs of Bodmin Moor
than any other photographer alive or dead. Here he demonstrates
his sense of geometry at the Cheesewring high above the Moor.
Kay Isbell's presence gives a sense of scale to this morning scene.

One old quarryman was convinced it was a relic of the Biblical Deluge. Some say it has a beautifully peaceful atmosphere, but others speak of strange sounds which defy rational explanation. 'The Cheesewring was indisputably once a witch's initiation rock . . .' That is the opinion of Peter Underwood, Life President of the Ghost Club Society.

From high ground like this, with the landscape stretching out like a living map, you begin to understand Cornwall is a draughtsman's country.

The Cheesewring is part of a famous ley line, beginning in Cornwall and ending in East Anglia. Some researchers believe the leys may, in fact, follow invisible lines of power criss-crossing the landscape. On a diamond-sharp day there are memorable views from Stowe Hill over the Tamar Valley to the east and out upon the moors to the west.

On good days you get a lovely light on Bodmin Moor, thrown up on the northern and southern flanks from the sea, and it is this quality of light which attracts painters and photographers. The moor too has inspired some fine writing. One thinks of the novels of Daphne du Maurier and, more recently, E V Thompson who lived for some years in an old miner's cottage not far from the Cheesewring. Ernest Thompson came to literary prominence through his bestselling novel *Chase The Wind* which won the 'Best Historical Novel Competition' in 1977. It is set on these beautiful but brooding moors.

In his book *Discovering Bodmin Moor*, first published by Bossiney in 1980, Ernest Thompson writes on his opening page:

'There is something indefinably romantic about a large tract of beautiful, windswept countryside, rich in history and legend, lying empty and almost unknown in the middle of England's most popular holiday county. Especially if that stretch of land is being gradually eroded by progress.

'Bodmin Moor is just such a place. It has been at the heart of all that is Cornwall since man made his first primitive home here almost 7,000 years ago.

'...To strike out across the coarse grass, leaving behind the grey stone moorside hamlets, is to stride back into history. Almost every age of man has left its brief mark here.'

■ THE PASTY and Cornwall go together naturally – like roast beef and Yorkshire pudding, or Gilbert and Sullivan.

But sadly no food has been so run down, so badly imitated as the Cornish pasty. The worst disasters tend to be commercial – some shops and cafes failing to ask a realistic price for the real thing. Instead they produce appalling imitations. The result is an insult to Cornwall, the Cornish and the pasty.

Historically, the first pasties were cooked in the late 1700s for the lower orders. The march of time and good sense in Cornish kitchens, however, combined to improve the quality, and in its heyday the pasty was a complete meal; meat and vegetables at one end, and apples and clotted cream at the other.

Miners in particular valued the Cornish pasty: though for some strange superstitious reason Cornish fishermen were loth to take a pasty to sea – or saffron cake for that matter. In the mines, there was a strange little tradition in the old days, in that a miner was always supposed to leave a 'corner' of his pasty for the 'knockers', as the evil spirits were called. It must have been a terrible temptation because many of us think the 'corner' is the best bit.

There is, however, still pride in the pasty – a good number of shops and cafes in Cornwall do produce the real thing, and, of course, many Cornish housewives know the knack of making and cooking a pasty – a meal of taste and quality. One such lady is Edna Ferrett who lives at Tintagel. Here are some wise words from Edna on the subject:

'A lot depends on your pastry, and there are just some times when it doesn't come out as right as you would like. Personally, I use plain flour with a mixture of lard and margarine, and preferably I make the pastry a day or so before I make the pasty. It somehow makes all the difference. A good bit of meat...that's essential...I don't necessarily say steak, but something of quality that will add gravy and improve the taste of the pasty...and you can add kidney because that too improves what I call the gravy quality of the meal. As a family, we like potato and plenty of onion, but that can be an acquired taste. We like plenty of seasoning, but people vary.'

Ray's photograph, captioned 'Cornish pasties with a smile' appeared in the old *Cornish Magazine* of September 1969. It shows Oscar Spry producing a fine harvest of pasties at the Swiss Bakery at Rock. Ray recalls: 'I often took the children down to the beach at Rock on a Saturday morning and on the way we bought pasties there. The establishment was run by a Mr Gartman, who came from Switzerland, hence the name. In addition to their pasties, they also produced excellent wholemeal bread.'

Young Cornish cooks.

■ TODAY Wenna Bishop, Ray's daughter, is a partner in Tamar Glass, a glass blowing workshop she started in 1993 with Andrew Potter and David Wall. Set in the peaceful countryside at North Petherwin near Launceston, this is the first glassworks of its kind to be founded in Cornwall for many years.

Wenna studied glass at the Royal College of Art in London, where she gained her MA in 1989. Then she ran a glass cutting workshop in the capital. Wenna has taken part in exhibitions in Bern, Switzerland, New Jersey, USA, Kensington, London and Liverpool.

In 1989 she was the Dudley Crystal Prize Winner at Broadfield House, Glass Museum, Stourbridge.

Of her return to Cornwall she says 'I had always intended to return to Cornwall at some point in my life, especially if I was to have children, as London had become so dangerous and dirty in the past few years. I did not expect the opportunity to come up quite so suddenly as it did to bring me back, salmon-like, to North Cornwall.'

Here her father photographs two examples of her work.

■ IT IS hard for us to think of Newquay as a village. In the Middle Ages though, it was a village called Towan Blistra, where the inhabitants lived, in the main, through fishing. The industry needed a quay to make a harbour, and one was built. As a result, the place began to be called 'New Quay' as early as the 1500s. Here is the Huer's Hut at Newquay on a stormy day in February 1970. Pilchards came in huge numbers and were caught with seine nets. Huers on the cliffs would watch for the shoals which they saw as 'a reddish discolouration of the sea,' and would cry 'Heva! Heva!' to warn their fellow villagers. The Huer would direct the boats to the shoals by signals from the cliff tops. However, towards the end of the nineteenth century, the pilchards disappeared from our Cornish waters and the livelihood of Newquay went with them, although a certain amount of shipbuilding continued. Fortunately for the economy, holidaymakers began to discover the glories of the northern coastline and its beaches, and with the coming of the railway in 1875 the real growth of the resort started.

■ *DRAMA at Wadebridge: a fire at the Mill Auto Supplies, evening, October 1993. Since then the store has been rebuilt.*

■ JETHRO is known as 'the world's funniest Cornishman.'

The son of a farmer, he has a magnificent Cornish accent and a barrel-full of entertaining stories. Here Ray photographs the Cornish comedian at cross-roads near St Breock. Jethro recalls: 'When I was working as a young man in a pub, I'd give away this photograph and tell the visitors if they had a wet day and couldn't go on the beach, then find these cross-roads.'

A keen sportsman, he plays golf on the beautiful but testing course at St Enodoc alongside the River Camel. In his younger days he played Rugby for the Pirates of Penzance & Newlyn, at prop forward, often alongside the England international Stack Stevens.

Jethro started his entertainments career in Cornish pubs – earlier he trained as a carpenter and after his apprenticeship went to work in a Cornish tin mine. Within a matter of months as a bar entertainer, he was recognised as Cornwall's top comedian, a man with a style all of his own.

He has appeared on many TV programmes, including Wogan, Jim Davidson Special – Jim rates Jethro his favourite storyteller – and hosted two shows of his own for HTV: 'The Jethro Junction.' In November 1990 he first appeared on the Des O'Connor Tonight show and later on Des O'Connor's Christmas Eve show, the only time any comedian had been invited back on the same series. After the popularity of these appearances on the small screen, there were no nights at home for Jethro. He was now appearing at clubs, private functions and sold-out theatres from the depths of Cornwall up to Manchester and the Lake District.

June 9 1991 was a notable night for the Cornishman: 'Jethro's Night of a Thousand Laughs' at the Cornwall Coliseum included guests Jim Davidson, Marti Caine, Jim Bowen, The Wurzels, Brian Conley, Karen Noble and the late Johnny Walker. The show was a tremendous success, raising a great deal of money for The Sharon Allen Leukaemia Trust and Treliske Hospital Haematology Department.

The rest, as they say, is show business history: packing major theatres throughout the UK, more appearances on TV with Des O'Connor and BBC Pebble Mill. In the summer season, he often splits his dates. In 1992 Jethro was making them laugh at Paignton,

Weston-super-Mare and Ilfracombe, and the following year there was another hectic summer programme: two nights at Bournemouth, two at Weston-super-Mare and three at Paignton.

As well as his travelling and storytelling, Jethro runs his own club just over the Tamar in Devon, and his video 'A Portion of Jethro' sold nearly 150,000 copies. Not for nothing has he been called 'The Prince of Cornish Wit.'

■ *JUNIOR members of the St Breward Band about to play on the Town Platt, Port Isaac, August 1971. They are, back row – left to right: Martin Fisher, Keith Babb, Philip Blake, Mike Rowe, Philip Hunt, and Gary Champion. Front row – left to right: Gillian Champion, Ann Rowe, Alison Skinner, Angela Fisher, Val Nottle and Margaret Rowe. The Band continues to play at Port Isaac on Thursdays through the summer season. All the girls are now maried, but two of the boys have gone on playing: Philip Blake is with the SWEB Camborne Band, and Mike Rowe loyally plays on for the St Breward Band. St Breward Silver Band has a long history. Formed in 1899, it has been making music ever since except for the 1914-18 and 1939-45 wars.*

■ NORTH Cornwall jollification by the Trevanson WI at Wadebridge Town Hall. Margaret Clapp, a long-time member of the WI, gave us the story behind this picture: 'I attended a meeting, where we had to discuss the arrangements for a WI group meeting, an event when we, as hosts, had to provide the speaker, the supper *and* the entertainment. I'd just been down to Carn Brea where they had staged 'The Last Night of the Proms,' with Benjamin Luxon, and it grew from there. Mrs Janet Townsend, the conductor of the Port Isaac Singers, offered to help us and she trained us to sing the Last Night of Proms songs. We had a podium made for Mrs Townsend, and the rest of the members came as Promenaders. There were flags and rattles and a banner saying 'Last Night of the Proms,' and the ladies wore red, white and blue. The whole thing really took off, the Promenaders joining in immediately, and we had some girls from Jenny Warwick's School of Dancing who danced the Hornpipe. It was a wonderful fun occasion.'

■ ANTHEA Barker, a Bossiney publishing colleague, sheltering from the invisible knife of the wind on a cold but sunlit Saturday morning in winter. Alex Tor is one of those beautiful but lesser known tors on the Moor; just above St Breward, it has unforgettable views for miles. In remoter parts of the moor you sometimes feel at the edge of the unknown.

A certain Mr Gilpin, an eighteenth century visitor to ancient Kernow dismissed Bodmin Moor in fifteen words: 'a barren and naked country, in all respects as uninteresting as can well be conceived.' Ray's photographs of the contrast and the beauty of the area show these words to be wildly inaccurate. Ray's shot of Alex was taken on a first visit to the tor in 1993. 'You *think* you know the Moor, but you go on discovering ...'

Bodmin Moor, the best known of our Cornish Moors, stretches twelve miles north to south and eleven miles east to west – small, of course, when you think of Dartmoor spreading itself over 365 square miles. But it has wonderful variety: changes in landscape and mood, and area steeped in history and folklore. Here the twentieth century and distant past merge to a curious tapestry – in places it is difficult to disentangle past from present or fact from fiction.

No-one can ever say he or she really *knows* the Moor, for the Moor may give us much – but only so much. There are *always* revelations in store.

■ *A FAMOUS stone circle or, more precisely, ring of stone: the Hurlers on the eastern edge of Bodmin Moor. Kay Isbell, who lives at nearby St Cleer, adds human interest to this photograph taken in 1988. Peter Underwood, who has been exploring the supernatural world for more than forty years, has ventured these thoughts: '...there is persistent evidence from different people that some stone circles, and the Hurlers in particular are "charged up" in some way and can give people who lean against them a distinct "shock." '*

*Cornish folklore has it that some athletic young men played the ancient Cornish sport of hurling on a Sunday and were turned to stone for their sins. Ray, who has photographed nearly all the stone circles in Cornwall, usually achieves his best results by standing on a stepladder – as he did on this occasion. 'It's necessary to get **above** the stones to get their real quality. From the ground they often appear just a jumble of stones and if you're high up in the air in a plane or helicopter they can look very flat . . . but a stepladder is just about right for the job.'*

■ NO, not a scene from the tropics. It's a bowls match on the Wadebridge green in September 1989. There is interesting speculation about the origin of bowls. Some believe it evolved from days of early history, when primitive man, in moments of relaxation, threw rocks or large stones at smaller stones or other targets. Its existence as a disciplined game may be safely tracked back some 7,000 years! Here at Wadebridge they have been playing bowls since around 1920. The first games were played in an area known locally as 'Piggy Lane', and then a second green was established at Egloshayle Playing Field – in what is today the children's play area. The third and present green, shown in this photograph, was made in the autumn of 1960 and the spring of 1961, and has been in use ever since. Mr Eddie Chapman, a local business man and keen bowler, who played for Cornwall, had the considerable honour of becoming the president of the England Bowling Association.

■ MARY Martin, one of our most distinguished native painters today, discussing one of her paintings at the North Cornwall Museum and Art Gallery, Camelford. This one-painter exhibition was staged by Sally Holden, on the right, the proprietor and curator, who lives at Delabole.

Opened in 1974, this privately-owned Museum is set in a building that was originally used for making coaches and wagons. The Museum covers many aspects of life in North Cornwall from fifty to a hundred years ago.

A prolific painter, Mary Martin often works on five or six paintings at the same time. When the first light of day seeps across the Cornish landscape, when most people are still in bed or only beginning to think about the day ahead, she is often already at work.

Her exhibitions, as on this occasion, are usually a Cornish celebration of colour and vitality. Hers is a mastery of the landscape she loves, from delicate detail like flowers in the foreground through sweeping vistas. She seems incapable of painting a dull picture and, above all, she captures this wonderful Cornish light. Through her eyes and her paintings you begin to understand better.

The Tamar Valley is Mary Martin country, but here in North Cornwall we are fortunate to have this important shop window for painters, potters and sculptors.

■ HEATHER Swain, who lives at Newhall Green near St Teath, is a well-known and highly popular potter in North Cornwall. Her pottery is full of fun and colour: teapots and butter dishes, bowls and jugs, egg-cups and candle holders. She brings the Cornish countryside into people's homes. Each item is hand-thrown in earthenware clay and hand-painted, humorously depicting animals in appealing settings. All pieces are covered in a transparent glaze and fired to seal the surface leaving them dishwasher and oven proof.

Heather, who trained in ceramic design at the West of England College of Art in Bristol, has lived in Cornwall for twenty years, and cares deeply about the landscape. She supplies pottery to Jane Churchill Ltd which has six prestigious shops in and around London. 'I'm doing work to blend in with their interiors, their range of wall paper and fabrics.'

Here Heather Swain is photographed at Minster, the Mother Church of Boscastle.

Whether you approach it from the climbing path through Minster Woods or via the lane linking Boscastle and Lesnewth, it comes as a delightful surprise. Set in an amphitheatre of trees, stately ivy-coated ashes and sycamores, the setting is almost too pretty to be true, particularly in the spring when daffodils and bluebells splash their colours over the old churchyard. And a surprise is that the saddleback tower appears unexpectedly below the level of the land. There is no hamlet of Minster, not a house in sight, the last place that you might expect to find a church. Actually the daffodils were the brain child of the Rev Bernard Lowe, who had the seeds sown during the Great War. An enterprising cleric, he wrote and published penny books of prayer that were read all over the country.

■ THEY say 'Every picture tells a story.' Well, yes and no. Truth is there is more than one story behind this photograph. Taken in 1972, it shows the then Mayor of Padstow, Gordon Dawe, speaking at an occasion celebrating two important sons of Padstow. They are Stephen Fuller, who in his tragically short life, worked unstintingly for Padstow and Cornwall, and Claude Berry, author, broadcaster and journalist. A reporter for the *Cornish Guardian*, Claude Berry spent six years in Fleet Street before returning to his native Cornwall. He was for many years the editor of the *West Briton*.

His widow, Mrs Winifred Berry, is seated on the chair and behind her is the distinguished Cornish historian, scholar and poet Dr A L Rowse who unveiled the plaque in Claude Berry's memory. The Cornish Bard Ernest Morton Nance, in kilt, paid tribute to Stephen Fuller – the seat here is in Stephen's memory. Another

Cornish Bard, Stephen Fuller was the creator and driving force of the *Padstow Echo* and a tireless ambassador for the port.

Ray has vivid memories of this event. He recalls, with a chuckle: 'I had taken my two children to the beach at Harlyn Bay, where we all changed into swimming gear as it was a very hot day. At the appropriate time I returned to the car, leaving the children to enjoy the sun and the sand, taking with me my bag of clothes which I would don in the car park at Padstow. When I got there I opened the bag and found that, in error, I'd taken the children's clothes, not my own. There was no time to return to Harlyn Bay and I had to take these official photographs wearing just my swimming trunks!'

ANOTHER example of Ray's ability to see and seize 'the moment.' He simply captions this 'Handfeeding gulls at Newquay.'

■ 'FROM Hartland Point to Padstow Light
Is a watery grave both by day and by night.'
Robert Stephen Hawker caught the grim reality in just two lines.
You have only to look at those graves of drowned sailors in his
churchyard at Morwenstow to know he wrote *the truth*. This beautiful but wicked coastline is littered with wrecks. Though these
cliffs wear storms well, they have a certain defiance, almost as if
they are defying and despising humanity and the full force of the
Atlantic.

In an age obsessed with progress and materialism, it is a relief
and release to stand on our North Cornish cliffs. North Cornwall
can be a great edge of tl.e ocean experience – and don't be put off
by what we call bad weather, days when J M W Turner painted
some of his most memorable pictures.

This coastline is saturated in history and legend. The exploits of
the smugglers alone would be worth a full book; illicit deeds
stained with blood and violence. Yet smuggling embraced all levels
of North Cornwall society, and in its heyday was a great Cornish
industry – and we must not think smuggling belongs exclusively to
the distant past. Ken Duxbury in his chapter in *Secret Cornwall* tells
the curious tale of a smuggling operation that went wrong – and
that was only ten years or so ago. A little matter of a waterproof
black box containing pure cocaine powder worth more than half a
million pounds!

Mermaids featured in old Cornish tales before the coming of
Christianity. Then they were said to be symbols of Aphrodite, the
Goddess of Love. Later, when the Cornish Mystery plays arrived
on the scene in the Middle Ages, the mermaid's personality
changed, portraying the two sides of Christ: half God and half man
just as she is half woman and half fish.

There is, in fact, a mermaid story surrounding that dangerous
sandbank at the mouth of the Camel Estuary, known as Doom Bar.
One theory is a local fisherman shot a mermaid with his arrow, and,
as an act of revenge, she cursed Padstow Harbour by putting this
sandbar across the entrance.

Here are some of Ray's coastal images.

■ *OUT of season on the north coast. This is the best time in the calendar for exploring this jagged coastline.*

■ THE ROAR of the sea: rough seas on Greenaway Rocks between Daymer and Polzeath.

The changing face of the Atlantic has challenged painters and photographers – the sheer scale and variety of the ocean. Romantic and mysterious yes, but in wild weather it can be simply full of terror and menace. Then a day later the sun can shine, and the sea sparkles – and boats glide gently on their way. In the words of Denys Val Baker: 'Isn't that really what makes Cornwall so rare and wonderful and magical a place?'

This stretch of coastline has, in fact, triggered one novel.

Sabine Baring-Gould, squire and parson for so long at Lewtrenchard just beyond Launceston, and author of that famous hymn *Onward Christian Soldiers*, set his novel *In the Roar of the Sea* here at Polzeath. It is a racy tale of dark nights and darker deeds: a mixture of wrecking and plunder. Its heroine is eighteen-year-old Judith Trevisa who desperately tried to protect her brother from evil influences. She alone dared to defy Captain Coppinger, the man they called Cruel Coppinger. There are many better novels in the Cornish library, but it is a 'good read'. The story of Cruel Coppinger is thought to be based on fact.

■ *PROFILE Rock at Boscastle, whose features from certain angles, uncannily resemble Queen Victoria.*

■ NEVIL Northey Burnard was a gifted Cornish sculptor. Here is his carving of John Wesley's head above the door of the old Methodist Meeting House in the village of Altarnun. Burnard, the son of the local stonemason, was born here in 1818, three years after Wellington and Waterloo. He was a mere sixteen-year-old when he did this work of the Methodist preacher. Burnard looked set for a golden career. At the pinnacle of his London days, he dined with the Queen and was feted by society, but the death of his young daughter Lottie shattered him, and, turning his back on the capital, he came back to Cornwall.

Mary Martin, that very fine painter from the Tamar Valley, has written a highly acclaimed and deeply sensitive publication on him: *A Wayward Genius*, published by Lodenek Press back in 1978. In Mary's words: 'There was a tragic dualism in Burnard's nature which underlay his rise and fall "from rags to rags."'

■ *BURNARD's birthplace in the village of Altarnun.*

Burnard's earthly end was truly tragic: a pauper's death in Redruth Workhouse in 1878. For more then seventy years, his grave remained unmarked in Camborne churchyard.

As for John Wesley, he must have been an experienced horseman, riding over 250,000 miles, sometimes covering 70 miles and preaching three sermons in the same day. In all, he preached more than 45,000 sermons – some of them before hostile assemblies. Even here in Cornwall he had to cope with the occasional riot.

There is a splendid story concerning the old Methodist Meeting House here at Altarnun. According to Lionel Pooley, a prominent local Methodist and a letter dated 2nd March 1868: Midway through a meeting one evening, the beam slipped out of the wall, sending the floor and all assembled crashing into the stabling below. An eye-witness recalled that some were calling out: 'Where is my dear sister?' and some were calling out 'Where is my dear brother?' and others: 'Where is my dear husband?' but nobody was asking: 'Where is my dear wife?' At the time of the accident a pub, called The Ring of Bells, stood next door. Hearing the noise, the landlord dashed from his bar, and standing at the entrance of the stabling called out: 'I see the Devil have got 'ee!'

▶

■ *TINTAGEL Pottery operates in the historic setting of Bossiney Court, a Norman Manor in Sir Francis Drake's former constituency.*

The pottery started life here in 1951 under the leadership of talented Pip Everard. Appropriately for a new Cornish venture, it took for its decorative ware motifs and symbols from the Celtic Druid times – and that tradition continues to this day.

In the words of the pottery's brochure:

'In a few strokes these motifs spell out the story of the human race – evolution from the mere animal to the thinking man – the spiral, for example, rising from earth to sky symbolizing the ascent from matter to mind. Man

76

himself is represented by a straight upward stroke and Woman as a circle. The colours portray the varying vibrations of the life force animating Man. The waving line, used in certain borders, emphasises again this eternal, unbroken progress, holding in its folds the egg of fertility.

'The apples, displayed in our dishes, are closely connected with the legendary King Arthur recalling the Isle of Averacht, or Isle of Apples, to which Arthur's body was taken by the mysterious Queen after he had been slain by the treacherous Mordred. The dragon symbol is also related to Arthur. Uther of Pendragon, mythical father of the Celtic King, took many shapes but chiefly the dragon. And through the centuries it has been a benevolent symbol, bringing with it prosperity and happiness in home, the fulfilment, in fact, of Man's hopes and ambition.'

This picture, taken in March 1969, shows Enid Mutton decorating a bowl with the traditional Tintagel dragon design. Enid Mutton, who has worked here since the opening day, has run the business in partnership with Roger Howard, since 1973. Watching her at work on this occasion is John Pardoe, the former Liberal MP for North Cornwall.

■ *GETTING good photographs, especially for the press, isn't a matter of luck. Often it's a network of contacts and friends feeding in information. This dramatic photograph of a crane tipped over at Padstow is such a case. Ray received a phone call from David Farquhar of Padstow telling him of the incident, and, as a result, hurried off to get this exclusive. David Farquhar, the man in the foreground, walking towards the camera, was a former Padstow to Rock ferryman and later a bookseller at The Strand: a great character of the old sea port. An old advertisement in Padstow Museum, announcing the 'Obby 'Oss ceremonies, states: 'led by our Dave.' 'That's me,' David Farquhar told us, 'I started carrying the 'Oss when I was only fifteen, and, in all, carried it for twenty-five years. When I started the 'Oss was weighing around two hundred pounds. Back in 1943 I carried it all day. Normally you carry the 'Oss in bursts of about twenty minutes to half-an-hour. I certainly knew all about it that year...why next day I had to go to the Doctor to have my shoulder stitched . . . had to have six or seven stitches where the shoulder straps had bitten into the flesh.' His mother, who was born at nearby Hawker's Cove, was accordionist on the great day, incredibly until she was eighty-one; while his father, a Scot and seaman, also contributed to the occasion. In Padstow Museum you can see a splendid Blue Ribbon 'Obby 'Oss cap, made by Mr Farquhar Senior, which was used from 1946 until 1968.*

■ OLD photographs of the Bush Inn, Morwenstow, show a fine old thatched roof, but sadly a fire in 1968 destroyed that grand roof and approximately half this ancient inn. Incredibly though today it retains the atmosphere of earlier times – and a genuinely haunted reputation.

Jim Gregory, the landlord here for many years, faces the camera. When the Ghost Club Society did a tour of haunted locations in North Cornwall in May 1994, members paid a visit to the inn, and Jim gave them some interesting paranormal accounts. Some people claim to have seen a dark shadowy figure moving away from the blazing building in 1968.

'I was assured it wasn't a billow of smoke, it had too much substance for that . . . I'm not saying it was a spirit or a ghost but the interesting thing is that we had had lots of strange happenings up to the date of the fire . . . and it seemed that the fire killed them off – or almost. Several people claim to have had unusual experiences here, and we, ourselves, had heard footsteps upstairs and on the staircase when we knew there was no-one about who could possibly make such noises. We had, over the years, a real floor show of noises, for which there was no rational explanation. For a time we

thought the fire had really removed this spirit, but then an American lady guest went to her room and discovered an elderly seafaring character, dressed in old-fashioned clothes. "What are you doing here?" she asked. But without replying, he turned and simply vanished through the wall!'

A clergyman friend of the family who often came to stay was put into the best room in the inn, but he asked to be moved. 'I feel menaced at night,' he explained. 'I can't sleep in that room.' He saw a shape and felt its presence leaning over the bed.

Since then, there has been a host of happenings defying logic. During a radio broadcast strange inexplicable noises were recorded, and during the interview the resident cat seemed to be picking up unseen presences. Less than twenty minutes after the interviewers left, Jim reported 'A whole floorshow of noises started. It were as if the spirit was saying "They've gone!"'

Jim Gregory also told us the curious history of an inn door. Morning after morning he found this particular door open. In an attempt to solve the problem, Jim put some wire around the catch – he thought it might be a cat using its paw to pull the catch down. But the door continued to be open next morning; so Jim used stronger wire. It still didn't work. He then put three turns of thick wire around the catch. The door was still open next morning – 'and the piece of wire was off!' Next night he used pliers, and twisting the wires round and round, said to himself: 'Now nothing will get it . . .' But next morning 'the damn wire was untwisted and the door open.'

We asked Jim some very specific questions about the mystery of the door. There was nothing vague or doubtful about his replies: 'It happened usually at five in the morning, or five in the evening. I've heard footsteps coming up the corridor. I've had the light on, and I've been standing here literally waiting for whatever it was to come through the door . . .'

'You have actually seen the door open?'

'Yes, I've seen the door open when it was shut and when the catch was wedged down.'

■ *THE WADEBRIDGE bypass bridge, almost completed, seen from the boatyard below. The completed bypass was opened on July 8 1993 by Robert Key MP, the then Minister for Roads and Traffic, whose father was a former Bishop of Truro. The bridge, which spans the River Camel, cost more than £4-million – money well spent in the eyes of many North Cornwall people because traffic jams in the town had been notorious for many years. The main 4km bypass involved the excavation of some 323,000 square metres of rock and shale, the laying of over 7,400 cubic metres of concrete and more than 100 miles of pre-stressing cable linking the eight piers of the bridge, which itself is approximately 20 metres high at the centre point.*

When we drive along this road we will never see the internal construction of the new bridge, but engineers will inspect it at frequent intervals. A special tunnel has been constructed underneath the roadway enabling them to study any stresses and strains in the structure.

■ JEAN Stubbs, the distinguished Cornwall-based novelist, at Lanhydrock, the beautiful National Trust property near Bodmin, when she was researching her book *Great Houses of Cornwall*. Born and brought up in Lancashire, the land of *The Guardian* and Sir

Neville Cardus, Old Trafford and cricket, Jean Stubbs has lived and worked in Cornwall since 1975. She was one of the first writers in the country to have a micro computer word processor which she finds invaluable for banking research and editing manuscripts. In 1984 she was appointed Writer in Residence for Avon. Her novels and short stories have been translated into eight languages and have been televised and adapted for radio. She and her husband Roy live in a two-hundred-year-old cottage at Nancegollan near Helston.

In a recent interview with the *Western Morning News*, she was asked 'Who, or what, apart from your family, do you care most about?' 'Old friends. Old houses,' she replied. 'The very young. The Dalai Lama. Music. Theatre. Writings of all kinds. Beauty in people and places and things. The light at particular times and seasons. Good food, good company, good conversation. Our cats. Our cottage.'

A very disciplined author, Jean Stubbs writes exactly 500 words each day on her world processor. Ivor Brown once said: 'To create eagerness is the function of the novelist.' Jean Stubbs generates that very quality, compelling us to read on – and turn the page. She truly belongs to Cornwall and is part of our great literary tradition – like Virginia Woolf and Dame Daphne du Maurier.

Her novel *Summer Secrets* inspired one reviewer to write: 'A rich, beautifully devised family history ... it will make you cry and laugh ... just like real life.' All her books are published by Macmillan and her latest, *Charades*, features a beautiful country house called Minions in Cornwall.

■ MORWENSTOW, of course is Parson Hawker Country.

Robert Stephen Hawker was at Morwenstow for more than forty years. He was more than a parson. He was a man who made things happen: he wrote poetry and prose, he built his famous vicarage here, he created the modern Harvest Festival service, he designed – in the form of a cross – the local school, and he gained immortality with *The Song of the Western Men* which has become the Cornish National Anthem. These are only *some* of his achievements in his legendary lifetime.

Here is his church, seen from the field on the seaward side. Hawker, like the Normans long before him, felt the power of the place – and left his mark upon it. Sir John Betjeman, visiting here, felt Hawker's 'strong Celtic, catholic and compassionate personality pervades this remote parish and particularly its church and glebe.'

There is a delightful story about the occasion when a rather pompous Archdeacon of Bodmin on a visit enquired: 'And what are your views, Mr Hawker?' The guest was promptly taken to the sitting room window and his host, with a familiar waft of the hand, declared: 'These are my views. My opinions I keep to myself!'

Hawker travelled hundreds of miles around North Cornwall with his favourite pony Carrow, sometimes ridden by his master and other times harnessed to a little vehicle.

On one dramatic occasion they were travelling from Welcombe back to Morwenstow and Hawker recalled: 'As I entered the Gulph between the Vallies today, a Storm leaped from the Sea, and rushed at me roaring – I recognised a Demon and put Carrow into a gallop and so escaped.'

Later in his ministry, though, he claimed genuine supernatural experience to the extent of *seeing* Saint Morwenna and, over the years, he became convinced in the power of the Evil Eye, once attributing the loss of nine suckling-pigs to a witch's curse. 'The sow which, like Medea, had taken a hatred to her own offspring, spurning them away from her milk...the evil eye of old Cherry (the witch) had turned the mother's heart to stone, and she let them die one by one...'

■ WHEN we think or talk of Jesus Christ, we come to the biggest mystery of all: God in human form, triumphing over the thing we call death and proving the reality of eternal Life. That has been the belief and conviction of millions of men and women, within the framework of the Christian faith, for a span of all but two thousand years.

And interestingly within a Cornish context we come to an absolutely fascinating question: Did Christ, as a boy, come to Cornwall?

There is a legend, bordering on a mixture of hope and belief, that the young Jesus did precisely that. There are various versions but the basic story is Jesus came to Cornwall with Joseph of Arimathea on a tin-buying venture. It is believed Joseph was an uncle of Mary, the mother of Jesus. Joseph was more than a wealthy trader and merchant, he was a skilful sailor and navigator. So it was natural he should suggest the boy Jesus should come with him on one of his voyages. And, of course, it is historically feasible.

After all, Blake, the mystic, wrote those stirring words:

And did those Feet in ancient time
Walk upon England's mountains green
And was the Holy Lamb of God
On England's pleasant pastures seen?

The North Cornwall version is that the boy Jesus came ashore at St Minver to get fresh water for the ship, and here you will find the only place on the map of Cornwall that bears his name. Standing in the middle of a field, Jesus Well still provides a water supply.

The Quiller Couches, on a visit in the 1890s, discovered that children suffering from whooping cough were still taken to drink the waters ... 'pins were dropped in for the telling of fortunes and even money was cast into its depths for the same reason ... one particular Sunday ... as much as sixteen shillings were taken out by unbelievers who then reaped the benefit of the superstitions of others.'

■ *RAY has an eye and a feel for the countryside. Here he captures a* ▶
nostalgic moment: a demonstration of steam ploughing.

■ A BREAK in film-making on the coast. This photograph is something of a mystery. Normally Ray keeps a meticulous record of all pictures taken, but this one slipped the net.

Ray thinks it may have been filming for the television version of *Jamaica Inn* because he has an idea the vessel became a shipwreck the following day in the story. Readers of the Daphne du Maurier novel will recall wrecking scenes.

Large tracts of Cornwall remain relatively unspoilt. Consequently film makers have been drawn here. The exotic silent film beauty Pola Negri is said to have caused 'unrest among the natives' in St Ives during the late 1920s.

Films, whether for television or the big screen of the cinema, have not only provided some wonderful entertainment, they have been powerful publicity boosts for tourism in the Westcountry.

Long may the cameras roll.

POSTSCRIPT

THESE pages are a panoramic view of life in and around North Cornwall – more than that they are a testament to the craft and awareness of *one* man.

Looking at the many magnificent pictures that have not been used though, brings two realizations.

First, these photographs are only a tiny fraction of Ray's prodigious output over the years. To do justice to the man, you would need to publish a thousand photographs. Secondly, production costs are such that we have been unable to convey his masterly technique of colour photography.

One person who does know something about Ray's colour photography is Elaine Beckton, who has handled Bossiney advertising for a number of years. Her company, Elaine Beckton Advertising, regularly features the covers of books in our advertisements and general promotion.

Elaine says: 'Despite advice not to, it is nevertheless widely acknowledged that we do indeed initially judge a book by its cover. It is therefore essential to capture the essence of the book on its cover, thus enticing the reader to explore the pages within. Ray Bishop's skilful use of the camera has produced many such book covers for Bossiney ... truly atmospheric reflections ... creative marketing at its best.'

MORE BOSSINEY BOOKS ...

SUPERNATURAL SEARCH IN CORNWALL
by Michael Williams
Investigates various facets of the paranormal in Cornwall.
'Fascinating reading.' Nancy Hammonds, *Evening Herald*

GHOSTLY ENCOUNTERS
by Peter Underwood, President of The Ghost Club
Six areas: Cornwall to Wiltshire: a whole range of haunted locations.
'... better read in broad daylight rather than in darkness.'
Frank Ruhrmund, *St Ives Times & Echo*

MYSTERIES OF THE SOUTH WEST
by Tamsin Thomas of BBC Radio Cornwall
A tour of ancient sites in Cornwall and on Dartmoor.
'There is little doubt that Tamsin Thomas has become the 'Voice of Cornwall'. Ronnie Hoyle, *North Cornwall Advertiser*

BODMIN MOOR THROUGH THE YEARS
by E.V. Thompson
'... a must for those who love the moor.'
The Western Morning News

LEGENDS OF CORNWALL
by Sally Jones

ABOUT PENZANCE
by Douglas Williams

MORE BOSSINEY BOOKS ...

WEST CORNWALL CAMERA
Photos by Harry Penhaul, text by Douglas Williams

EAST CORNWALL IN THE OLD DAYS
by Joy Wilson

ABOUT LAND'S END
by Wendy Lewis

ABOUT THE LIZARD
by Michael Williams

NORTH CORNWALL REFLECTIONS
by Hilda Hambly
'... *a treasure chest of nostalgia.*'   *Prime of Life*

SUPERNATURAL INVESTIGATION
by Michael Williams
'*A very nice collection of supernatural stories from the United Kingdom
... superbly illustrated.*'   *The Ghostbuster,* USA

SECRET CORNWALL
Introduced by Madeleine Gould of BBC Radio Cornwall
Seven writers make seven journeys.

TINTAGEL REFLECTIONS
by Felicity Young & Michael Williams

MORE BOSSINEY BOOKS ...

STRANGE TALES OF THE SOUTH WEST
by Ronnie Hoyle
The South West is a natural breeding ground for strange tales.
Well-known Westcountry journalist Ronnie Hoyle in his debut
for Bossiney confirms this eerie fact.

KING ARTHUR IN THE WEST
by Felicity Young & Michael Williams
'... *brings together many of the strands in an exploration which takes
them from Tintagel Castle and the Great Halls to Dunster and
Dozmary, Glastonbury and so many other centres.*'

The Western Morning News

MYSTERIES IN THE CORNISH LANDSCAPE
by Tamsin Thomas of Radio Cornwall
A tour of thirty historic locations in Cornwall by the well-known
Cornish broadcaster, starting at Chun Castle down in the
Hundred of Penwith and ending at The Hurlers on the eastern
edge of Bodmin Moor.
*'Tamsin takes us on an enjoyable and speculative canter – literally for
she is often on horseback – through these fascinating and often contro-
versial features of old Kernow.'* Donald Rawe, *Cornish Scene*
*'Tamsin has produced a delightful book which will enchant her audi-
ence.'* Ronnie Hoyle, *The Western Morning News*

We shall be pleased to send you our catalogue giving full details
of our growing list of titles of Devon, Cornwall, Dorset,
Somerset and Wiltshire and forthcoming publications. If you
have difficulty in obtaining our titles, write direct to Bossiney
Books, Land's End, St Teath, Bodmin, Cornwall.

■ *Back cover: The Cornish know how to celebrate and seize any excuse to have a good time. They keep the traditional customs like Mayday, the 'Obby 'Oss and hurling, there are still the chapel Sunday School outings and the church strawberry teas – but any new excuse for dressing up and putting on a good old-fashioned spread is welcomed by any community, large or small. Here, Padstow folk celebrate the Queen's Silver Jubilee with a street party in wonderful summer sunshine. Flowers decorate the little girls' hats, flags and garlands brighten the street. And then, naturally, there's the food . . .*